TWITTER

ABDO
Publishing Company

TECHNOLOGY
PIONEERS

TWITTER

THE COMPANY AND ITS FOUNDERS

by Christine Heppermann

Content Consultant
Anthony J. Rotolo
Professor of Practice,
Syracuse University iSchool

CREDITS

Published by ABDO Publishing Company, PO Box 398166, Minneapolis, MN 55439. Copyright © 2013 by Abdo Consulting Group, Inc. International copyrights reserved in all countries. No part of this book may be reproduced in any form without written permission from the publisher. The Essential Library™ is a trademark and logo of ABDO Publishing Company.

Printed in the United States of America,
North Mankato, Minnesota
052012
062013

 THIS BOOK CONTAINS AT LEAST 10% RECYCLED MATERIALS.

Editor: Megan Anderson
Series Designer: Emily Love

Library of Congress Cataloging-in-Publication Data
Heppermann, Christine.
  Twitter : the company and its founders / Christine Heppermann.
    p. cm. -- (Technology pioneers)
  ISBN 978-1-61783-337-3
  1. Twitter (Firm)--Juvenile literature. 2. Twitter--Juvenile literature. 3. Online social networks--United States--Juvenile literature. 4. Internet industry--United States--Juvenile literature. I. Title.
  HM743.T95H47 2013
  338.4'70046780973--dc23
                                        2012007218

TABLE OF CONTENTS

Janis Krums posted this photo of the Hudson plane landing to Twitter before any other media outlets arrived on the scene.

BREAKING NEWS

Janis Krums was too busy helping rescue passengers to think about the photo. US Airways Flight 1549 had crash-landed in the Hudson River only minutes earlier. When the ferryboat Krums was taking from Manhattan to New Jersey changed course and pulled close to the downed plane, he took a picture with his iPhone. He then posted the picture to the social networking Web site Twitter, along with a hurried tweet: "There's a plane in the Hudson. I'm on the ferry going to pick up the people. Crazy."[1]

It was January 15, 2009, a sunny, but cold winter day. Incredibly, all 155 people aboard the aircraft survived the crash. Now they needed to get out of the wind and frigid water before they developed hypothermia. Some passengers huddled in inflatable life rafts; others stood, drenched, on the right wing of the slowly submerging plane. The ferry, the first boat to reach the scene, headed for the wing. Krums pitched in to bring people to safety and provided warmth by giving his overcoat, gloves, and a couple of hats from his luggage to others.

WHAT IS A TWEET?

Tweet, like other terms in the Twitter vocabulary, was coined by Twitter users. As a noun, it refers to a single Twitter post, each of which is limited to 140 characters. In its verb form, it is used as in, "He tweeted the news about his promotion as he left the boss's office."

He also lent his phone to passengers so they could call loved ones and tell them they were okay. In the meantime, his photo had begun an incredible journey of its own.

AROUND THE WORLD IN MINUTES

Even though fewer than 200 Twitter users followed Krums's account, those followers looked at his photo and passed it along to other Internet users, who then shared it with others. Almost 40,000 Web users viewed the photo in the first four hours on TwitPic, a site where Twitter photos are hosted. At one point, TwitPic crashed because too many people attempted to simultaneously view Krums's unbelievable shot. Later reports revealed that Krums and fellow Twitter users broke the story of Flight 1549 a full 15 minutes before word appeared on

QUICK THINKING

The airplane crash made an international hero out of the plane's pilot, Captain Chesley B. Sullenberger. In an interview with Katie Couric on the television news program *60 Minutes*, the captain explained that his first reaction on realizing both of the plane's engines had failed "was one of disbelief."[2] But he quickly composed himself and put together a plan for an emergency water landing that saved the lives of everyone on the aircraft. Of the first responders, such as Krums, who arrived on boats to aid the survivors, Sullenberger said, "Thank you seems totally inadequate. I have a debt of gratitude that I fear I may never be able to repay."[3]

Krums posted the photo of the Hudson plane crash to TwitPic.

television or in any other traditional media venue. The first tweet about the event was written by New York City Twitter user Jim Hanrahan, which came in four minutes after the plane hit the water.

CITIZEN JOURNALISM

Technology has evolved to the point that anyone with a smartphone can be a news reporter. As Krums told an interviewer, "Traditional journalists will always be second on the scene from now on, especially in the developed world."[5] The public can watch stories unfold as they happen and are told by the people who are involved. Technology not only has changed how we report the news, it has changed the way we receive it. Gone are the days of sitting passively in front of a radio or television. Thanks to the Internet, says Krums, "People now interact with their news. You can get into an online community and start talking about a topic."[6] Of course, not every eyewitness is a reliable source, and traditional news outlets still have the advantage of fact-checking departments that can verify information before it goes out to the public. Yet, to a certain degree, the Internet gives everyone the opportunity to be a fact checker, to chime in on a story, and to comment on aspects of it that a reporter may have missed or gotten wrong. This type of communication happens at a speed unheard of. Prior to the Internet, it could take days or weeks for a reader's letter to the editor to appear in the paper. Now, the world is filled with citizen journalists who are always on the scene.

It read, "I just watched a plane crash into the hudson riv [sic] in manhattan."[4]

Krums was not the only passenger on the ferry who took a photo that day. But he was the only one who became famous for being a citizen journalist. This businessman from Sarasota, Florida, made history, but not because he took a photo. He made history because he tweeted it.

LITTLE DID THEY KNOW

According to the dictionary, the verb *twitter* means "to utter a succession of small, tremulous sounds, as a bird."[7] Jack Dorsey thought of the idea for a Web-based Short Message Service (SMS). That definition more or less describes what he envisioned—a steady stream of online chatter in which users could let friends and family members know what they were up to at any moment. "What are you doing?" was the question Twitter prompted its users to answer. When Dorsey composed and sent the first tweet on March 21, 2006, he answered the question with: "just setting up my twttr."[8] When the site first launched, the name of the service had no vowels, but the company soon added them.

At that time, critics wondered why anyone would care about this new form of social media. They considered Twitter to be a glut of mundane, useless information—a bunch of people chirping about

THE QUESTION CHANGES

In 2009, Twitter acknowledged that "What are you doing?" no longer reflected the many uses people had for the service, so they changed the official question to "What's happening?" A November 19, 2009, post on the company's blog noted, "Sure, someone in San Francisco may be answering 'What are you doing?' with 'Enjoying an excellent cup of coffee,' at this very moment. However, a birds-eye view of Twitter reveals that it's not exclusively about these personal musings. Between these cups of coffee, people are witnessing accidents, organizing events, sharing links, breaking news, reporting stuff their dad says, and so much more."[9]

what they were eating or buying or watching on television. Dorsey and his colleagues did not exactly dispute this evaluation. According to Twitter cofounder, Evan Williams, they compared the service to ice cream—more fun than useful.

In the beginning, Dorsey, Williams, their partner Christopher "Biz" Stone, and others who worked with them at the time never really considered all the things Twitter users might be doing that were not mundane and boring. For instance, users might be trying to steady themselves during an earthquake. They might be in the middle of a political uprising in Iran, Tunisia, or Egypt or part of a crowd of protestors working to overthrow a corrupt government. They might be witnessing a historic speech given by a newly elected president. They might be riding a ferry to New Jersey when a plane crashes into the Hudson River and changes their lives—and the lives of many others—forever.

More than a year after sending the tweet that made him famous, Krums participated in an online interview. He commented that he never imagined what a powerful tool this amusing, but seemingly inconsequential, application on his iPhone could be. "At that moment, I saw the value in what it was, but I didn't see the value in what it could become.

Biz Stone and Evan Williams helped launch
Twitter into a worldwide phenomenon.

I don't think anyone could see that it could be spread
around the world the way it was."[10] Today, Krums
has more than 11,000 Twitter followers.

Twitter has become a global community with
more than 500 million registered users around
the world. Twitter is a fitting accomplishment for

Jack Dorsey. As a boy growing up in Saint Louis, Missouri, Dorsey was fascinated with the bustle and hum of city life. His dream had always been to become the mayor of New York City. In the meantime, he created his own bustling, thriving, ever-growing metropolis online. +

Twitter cofounder Jack Dorsey had 1.8 million
Twitter followers as of March 2012.

Computers in the 1970s were a far cry from the handheld
devices used today.

BEFORE TWITTER

Not all that long ago, the Internet did not
exist—at least not in the form we know today.
In the 1960s, a US Department of Defense
agency known as Defense Advanced Research
Projects Agency (DARPA) began experimenting

to create a network that shared information by linking computers at several US universities and government agencies. This led to the creation of Advanced Research Projects Agency Network (ARPANET), a precursor to the Internet.

One key figure in the creation of the Internet was Dr. Leonard Kleinrock. As a graduate student at Massachusetts Institute of Technology (MIT), Kleinrock wrote a paper entitled "Information Flow in Large Communication Nets." This paper laid out his theory of "packet switching," the technology underlying the Internet. Kleinrock and his lab assistant made the first host-to-host ARPANET connection on October 25, 1969, in California between UCLA and Stanford Research Institute.

In 1971, researchers proposed the protocol Telnet as a way to connect computers remotely and run simple programs or read data. A protocol is an agreed-upon set of rules between two devices

PACKET SWITCHING

Packet switching refers to the transmission of data over a network by breaking down a message into smaller parts. Each part is sent individually and then reassembled into the original message once they reach their destination. When an e-mail is sent, the message leaves as a series of packets. Each packet contains information about the sender and the receiver to help it reach its destination. If an Internet browser is prompted to load a Web page, it arrives as a series of packets that the browser reassembles.

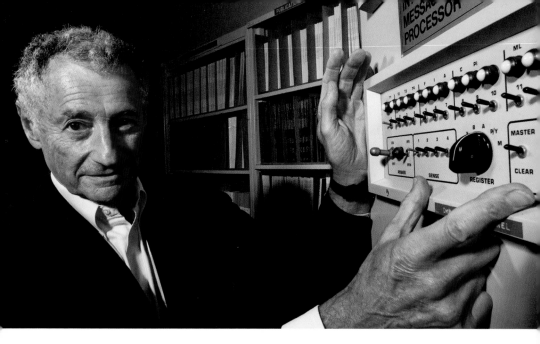

Dr. Leonard Kleinrock was a key figure in the development of the Internet.

that determines the format of data and how it is transmitted. The first version of Telnet, produced in 1983, was used to access games, library card catalogs, and other information. By 1991, Telnet could access weather information on the University of Michigan's Weather Underground. To do this, a person could log onto a computer and, at the command prompt, enter the command: telnet madlab.sprl.umich.edu:3000. This connected the computer, commonly through dial-up phone lines, to the University of Michigan. The user entered the name of a city and waited for a block of text to appear on the screen with that city's current forecast. At that time, there were no pictures or graphics, only text.

Another early staple of the Internet was File Transfer Protocol, or FTP, which allowed users to access remote computers and upload or download files. After entering a request to download a small image from an FTP, the image would be transferred from the FTP to the hard drive of the user's computer. If the computer had enough memory and the right software, the user could open and view the picture.

DIAL-UP

Technology advanced in the 1980s that allowed computers to communicate to other computers— to transmit and receive data—through dial-up connections. An electronic device called a modem facilitated these dial-up connections. Modems, which were fairly inexpensive and readily available for purchase in the 1980s, allowed for the transmission of data from one computer to another via telephone lines.

EARLY SOCIAL MEDIA

The first recognizable social media sites were bulletin board systems (BBSs) of the 1980s. Much like the rectangular cork bulletin boards in classrooms where teachers pinned student work or class announcements, BBSs provided virtual space for computer users to leave messages for one other. BBSs first started in the United States and eventually spread worldwide. BBS groups formed, organizing around different areas of interest such as politics, sports, or gaming. Early BBS groups were often localized and represented the first virtual communities. Some people met in person after interacting on the BBS. People who shared a passion for the latest software games could come together to trade software updates, strategy, and opinions.

WORLD WIDE WEB VS. THE INTERNET

It is common for people to use *World Wide Web* and *Internet* interchangeably. But technically, they are two different but related things.

The Internet refers to all of the computers that are connected together—all of the physical networks and the devices that link them—as well as the information that flows over these networks. There are many different ways to share data over the Internet, some of which are used primarily by researchers and corporations. For example, when Microsoft sends out a software update for Windows, it is installed automatically on computers; the software downloads over the Internet, not the World Wide Web.

The World Wide Web is a part of the Internet, the way a neighborhood is part of a city. To transmit data, the Web uses a language called hypertext transfer protocol (HTTP). The Web consists of information viewable in Web browsers such as Firefox or Internet Explorer. Often this information displays in a graphic format with many images on attractively designed Web pages. Whenever you use a Web browser to access the Internet, you are using the World Wide Web.

In the 1990s, as Internet usage branched into homes and workplaces, Web services specifically designed to allow people to socialize online emerged. The era of social media arguably began in 1997 with the launch of SixDegrees.com. This was the first site that offered users the chance to create personal profiles, amass a list of friends who were allowed to access those profiles, and peruse the friend lists of fellow users. However, SixDegrees.com did not last long and shut down in 2000. One of the reasons for its lack of success was its limited functionality, which made users lose interest. Users also complained that the site misused their contact information and sent SPAM messages to their e-mail addresses. But its founders believe SixDegrees.com was ahead of its time.

A BLIZZARD AND THE BBS

In 1978, IBM programmer Ward Christensen and fellow programmer Randy Seuss created the first BBS while they were snowed in by a January blizzard in Chicago, Illinois. With Christensen writing the software and Seuss configuring the hardware, they achieved their goal of creating an electronic version of the traditional bulletin board in just a few weeks. On February 16, 1978, the Computerized Bulletin Board System (CBBS) began operating. Christensen and Seuss's invention started a trend. Approximately 45,000 BBSs were in operation in the United States by 1992. In that year, the advent of the World Wide Web and Web sites made the BBS obsolete.

THE BIRTH OF BLOGS

The Web site LiveJournal.com launched in March 1999. LiveJournal had several characteristics in common with SixDegrees. Its users did not scribble their innermost thoughts into locked books kept hidden under their mattresses. Rather, they posted entries on the LiveJournal Web site where other users had the option to follow and comment on entries if they found them interesting.

LiveJournal helped popularize blogging, which was the universal term used for Web logging. With the launch of social networking sites that immediately thrived, such as Friendster (2002), MySpace (2003), and Facebook (2004), more people were starting to know their way around the Internet. +

Friendster was one of the first popular social networking Web sites.

Dorsey loved studying maps when he was a child.

FROM TAXICABS TO TWEETS

City maps covered the walls of Jack Dorsey's childhood bedroom. He loved to study the layout of a teeming urban area and figure out how everything fit together. As he later told a reporter for *Vanity Fair* magazine, "I wanted to

play with how the city worked, so I could see it."[1]
His favorite activity was wandering the streets of
downtown Saint Louis, but when he couldn't do that,
he pored over his maps, staring at an intersection of
two streets and imagining what was going on there at
that very moment.

Vehicles also fascinated him—police cars,
taxicabs, ambulances, and trains. He and his younger
brother, Danny, took a video camera to a local rail
yard to make movies of the trains as they rolled past.
But it was not really the physical appearance of a
train or taxi that captured young Jack's attention.
Instead, he admired the communication system. He
was obsessed with how a police car, for instance,
could radio its location from anywhere in the city
so when a crime was reported, headquarters knew
exactly which officers on patrol could get to the
scene the fastest. He relished the efficient language
cab drivers used to communicate their whereabouts
to dispatchers. To him, their brief radio messages
were almost like poetry.

COMPUTER WHIZ

Jack Dorsey was born November 19, 1976, to
parents Marcia and Tim. His family purchased their

Jack Dorsey's first computer was an IBM PC Jr.

first personal computer (PC)—an IBM PCjr—in 1984. Jack immediately demonstrated a talent for programming and could design maps of his own:

> *I taught myself how to program so I could draw a map. Then I drew some dots on the map, and then I figured out how to make the dots move around within the street boundaries.*[2]

With the dots, he traced the routes of police and paramedics responding to calls that he heard by listening to an emergency service radio scanner. Now, instead of a lifeless piece of paper, he had an interactive scene. It was as if he were watching the city of Saint Louis move and breathe before his very eyes.

Jack's mother owned a coffee shop. One day, a customer told her he needed to hire programmers for his software company. She recommended her oldest son. So, at age 15, Jack began working as a summer intern for Jim McKelvey, who became a good friend and eventual business partner. Today, McKelvey remembers that Jack's skill and shrewdness surpassed that of most of the adult employees. Once, when a colleague asked McKelvey for direction on a project, he replied, "Just do *everything* this kid says."[3]

In 1997, as a junior at the University of Missouri-Rolla, Jack landed his dream job in his dream

RADIO SCANNER

Radio scanners, similar to the one Jack Dorsey used to track emergency vehicles, are receivers that monitor different radio channels at the same time they search for signals. Also called police scanners, they are used by hobbyists, journalists, off-duty emergency service personnel, and crime investigators to stay aware of accident reports and criminal activity.

NEW YORK CITY TAXIS

When Jack Dorsey moved to New York City to design dispatch software, he was definitely in the right place. Among other operations, such as courier services and emergency vehicle coordination, New York City dispatchers presided over a fleet of more than 12,000 taxicabs that, like a swarm of bumble bees, buzz through traffic carrying more than 200 million passengers every year. Operated by private companies, cabs carry 25 percent of all fare-paying transit users and collect 45 percent of fares in Manhattan, and 30 percent of fares in the entire metropolitan area. Other fare-based modes of transportation include subways, buses, and private car services.

city. He had contacted DMS, the largest courier dispatch service in the world, to let them know about a loophole he had found in their online security. He then received an invitation from Greg Kidd, the company's Chief Executive Officer (CEO), to move to New York City and work for them. From Jack's perspective, nothing could be better than writing dispatch software and getting paid for it. He transferred to New York University and began juggling his college coursework with his job at DMS.

In 1998, Jack and Kidd relocated their business from New York to San Francisco. They hoped to add their dispatch service to the booming crop of Internet companies emerging in Silicon Valley. When their company folded almost as soon as it started, Jack found himself at loose ends. He did freelance work for other dispatch operations before moving back to Missouri, where he studied to become a massage therapist. He then returned to San Francisco and lived in an apartment behind Kidd's house and babysat for Kidd's daughter.

CONSTANT CONNECTION

Dorsey never lost his conviction that quick, easy, real-time messaging should be available to all. Years later, he described how the initial inspiration for Twitter grew from the simple, elegant pattern of dispatch communication, "Someone broadcasts a message, and those interested in it follow it, and that's it."[4] If this pattern worked so well

THE DOT-COM BOOM

During the second half of the 1990s, it seemed the Internet might fundamentally change the way we do business. Instead of shopping in physical stores, people were shopping online for everything from groceries to clothing to furniture. This belief in a new economy led investors to pay inflated prices for the stock of all companies that had any kind of Internet-related business model. Dorsey and Kidd looked to capitalize on the Internet boom by creating an online dispatch service company in San Francisco. Entrepreneurs started all manner of new companies and became rich seemingly overnight by selling stock at inflated prices.

Eventually the Internet bubble, as the media called it, burst. While some online businesses flourished, the majority went bankrupt because they did not have well thought-out business models. Computer programmers lost lucrative jobs and entrepreneurs who were temporary millionaires went broke. Investors who paid sky-high prices to get in on the stock boom saw their savings disappear. Experts who tried to convince the world the new economy had fundamentally different rules than the old economy became laughingstocks.

WHAT IS AN ENTREPRENEUR?

An entrepreneur is someone with an idea for a business or product who is willing to take financial and personal risks to turn that vision into reality. Famous American entrepreneurs include automobile manufacturer Henry Ford and inventor Thomas Edison. As an entrepreneur in the field of computer innovation, Dorsey joins the ranks of such notable figures as Bill Gates, cofounder of Microsoft computer company; Steve Jobs, cofounder of Apple Computers; and Mark Zuckerberg, creator of the social networking Web site Facebook.

for taxi and ambulance drivers, why couldn't it work for everybody? Why shouldn't he and his friends be able to keep in constant contact and have the ability to let each other know where they were and what they were doing at all times?

Dorsey initially tested this idea in 2000. For the first part of his test, Dorsey wrote some simple computer code. This code allowed him to compose an e-mail message and send it to a single address, which would then repost the message to the group of friends whose e-mail addresses he had entered into the program. Grabbing his BlackBerry 550, one of the first smartphones on the market, Dorsey went for a walk in San Francisco's Golden Gate Park. In the park's western section, a small herd of buffalo grazed in an enclosed field under the protection of the San Francisco Zoo. Using his BlackBerry, Dorsey wrote this

The Bison Paddock at Golden Gate Park in San Francisco

message and posted it to five of his friends: "I'm at the Bison Paddock watching the bison."[5] He quickly realized two things. None of his friends on the list had BlackBerrys, and none of them cared that he was at the Bison Paddock.

Today, Dorsey realizes that one of the key aspects of entrepreneurship is to know when the time is right. In 2000, the world did not see much use for real-time group messaging. But that did not mean he had to completely give up on his idea. "Build a thousand things and put them on a shelf," Dorsey advises. "Then watch and wait for the right opportunity to dust them off and pick them up again."[6]

Six years later, Dorsey's idea for a Web-based, real-time SMS came off the shelf. A lot had happened in the field of technology since that day at the Bison Paddock. More people in the United States had smartphones. More people had Internet access. Finally, it seemed, the time was right. +

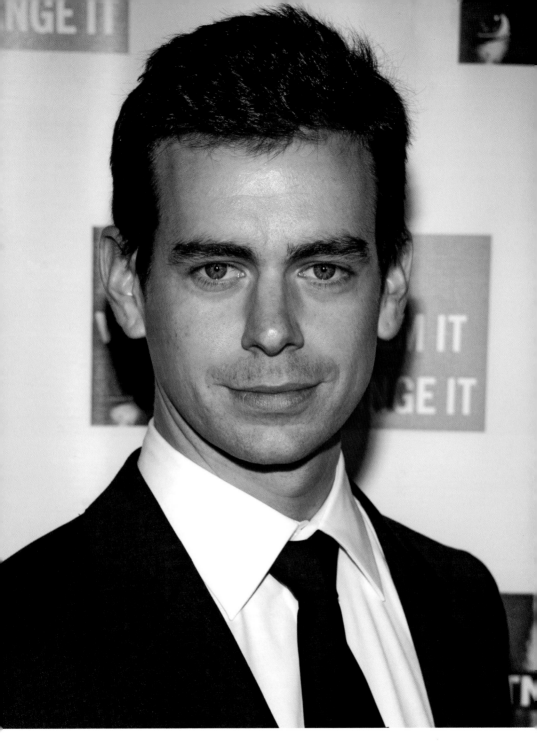

Increases in smartphone and Internet use made Dorsey's idea
for a SMS more practical.

Growing up on a farm in Nebraska, Evan Williams
dreamed of becoming an entrepreneur.

EVAN WILLIAMS
AND BIZ STONE

Evan Clark "Ev" Williams was born
March 31, 1972, on a farm near Clarks,
Nebraska, approximately 70 miles (113 km)
from Lincoln. Evan's family grew corn and soybeans.

During the summer, he was responsible for making sure the crops were irrigated.

Growing up, Evan did not fit in as the typical boy from Nebraska. He later told the *New York Times*:

> *I had a fierce desire to create things, to be independent and prove myself, which caused me to reject authority, but never in a sort of rebellious way. It was more like, 'I'm going to show you by doing it all myself.'*[1]

Evan attended the University of Nebraska at Lincoln, but dropped out after a year and a half. "I felt college was a waste of time; I wanted to start working," he said.[2] First he headed to Florida and did freelance copywriting. Next he landed in Texas, where he stayed with his older sister while he pondered his next move.

After returning to Nebraska in 1994, Evan started his first business in Lincoln, which was financed by his father. The company designed Web sites and produced CD-ROMs about Nebraska football. The business did not have much money and none of the employees knew how to write software. Evan said, "We watched what entrepreneurs in California were doing and tried to play along."[3]

CD-ROMs

CD-ROM is short for Compact Disc-Read-Only Memory. CD-ROMs were introduced in 1982 for digital audio reproduction, but could also be used to store data. A standard CD-ROM can hold 680 megabytes of memory, the equivalent of 300,000 text pages. CD-ROMs are read by CD-ROM drives on computers. CD-ROM drives became more and more common because CD-ROMs are a low-cost way for companies to store and distribute software programs and databases. To handle increasingly larger multimedia files, the digital videodisc (DVD) was introduced in 1995.

The business was a failure for Williams, who lacked focus, did not keep track of money well, and was unable to repay his father's investment. About his first business he wrote in the *New York Times*, "I had no business running a company at that time because I hadn't worked at a real company."[4]

CALIFORNIA BOUND

Poring over issues of *Wired* magazine, Williams dreamed of going to California and becoming an entrepreneur. With nothing to lose, in 1997 he headed west to Sebastopol, California. He took a job in marketing at O'Reilly Media, a technology publisher. Founder Tim O'Reilly described Williams as frustrated and wanting to do things differently. "He had a little bit of attitude, a chip on his shoulder, but always with good spirit," he told the *New York Times*.[5]

After seven months, Williams left O'Reilly to start Pyra Labs in January 1999. His cofounder was his former girlfriend Meg Hourihan. Williams's high school friend Paul Bausch soon joined them at Pyra. The company's first product was Pyra, a Web-based project management program for companies. One of its tools was a note-taking application, which as a side project Pyra Labs developed into a new company called Blogger in August 1999. Blogger became one of the first Web services that helped Internet users publish their own blogs.

BIZ STONE

Christopher Isaac "Biz" Stone was born March 10, 1974, and grew up in Wellesley, Massachusetts. Early on, Biz had a love for graphic arts

O'REILLY MEDIA

Tim O'Reilly founded O'Reilly & Associates in 1978. Now called O'Reilly Media, the company publishes educational books and magazines about computer technology topics. The company also produces conferences on technology topics. Based in Sebastopol, California, O'Reilly Media published the first popular book about the Internet in 1992, *The Whole Internet User's Guide & Catalog*. O'Reilly Media books are known for their black-and-white illustrations of animals on the covers. O'Reilly has published the quarterly magazine *Make: Technology on Your Time* since 2005. The magazine features articles on technology-related do-it-yourself projects.

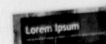

google.com https://www.google.com/accounts/Service

Blog +

Blogger

Create a blog. It's free.

Lorem Ipsum

Lorem Ipsum

Blogger made it easy for users to publish and update their own blogs.

and theater. He first studied writing at Northeastern University in Boston, Massachusetts, but dropped out after a year. "I just thought I had to go to college after high school," Stone told the *San Francisco Chronicle*. "No one ever told me I didn't have to."[6]

Biz then studied writing at the University of Massachusetts in Boston, but again dropped out after the first year. While still at the University of Massachusetts, he became a designer at publisher Little, Brown and Co.

Like Williams, Biz discovered he had a knack for Web design and programming. His friend Marc Ginsburg pitched him the idea for a social networking site called Xanga.com in 1999. Biz and Ginsburg launched the site in 2000, and Biz became creative director. "It looked a lot like MySpace before MySpace," Biz said. "It was a blogging community and got very popular very fast."[7]

Unhappy with Xanga's direction in 2001, Biz bounced back and forth between the East and West Coast. First he moved to Los Angeles, California, after his childhood friend Greg Yaitanes, an Emmy-winning television director, invited him to work in television. In 2002, he wrote a book titled *Blogging: Genius Strategies for Instant Web Content* and almost returned to publishing. Instead, Biz returned to the Boston area and worked for the Wellesley College alumni association.

Biz Stone has written two books about blogging.

LIFE AT GOOGLE

In 2003, Williams invited Stone to come work for Blogger, which Internet search engine company Google had just acquired. "It was a chance for me to get behind the screen again," Stone said.[8]

Williams and Stone worked at Google for 20 months, helping launch a redesign of Blogger during that time. But Williams decided to leave and Stone followed. The decision to leave was not an easy one, Stone said. "It was about the toughest decision I ever made," he said, "and if I'd known how high Google stock would go, I'm not sure I would have made it."[9]

Upon leaving Google, Williams helped start the company Odeo with his neighbor Noah Glass, and Stone joined him. Odeo was involved in designing software for podcasts.

DORSEY'S FIRST REAL JOB

Dorsey first met Williams and Stone while applying for a job at Odeo. Up to this point, Odeo had operated out of Glass's apartment. Dorsey submitted his resume to Williams, who was Odeo's CEO.

EVERYONE CAN BE AN AUTHOR

Longtime blogger Stone commented on the rush he felt after publishing his first blog entry in 1999: "There it was, my public blog. My words published on the Web. I was a writer and a web builder. My enthusiasm for this new medium . . . was immediate. I was excited, not only for myself but for what blogging could mean . . . this is the true democratization of the web. Everybody will have a voice here."[10]

Dorsey remembers this as the first time he had ever applied for a real job instead of just falling into opportunities through friends or online connections.

He may not have looked professional—he had piercings in both ears and his nose, and he wore his hair in dreadlocks—but anyone who had ever worked with him knew he took every project seriously.

Within a month after Dorsey came on board at Odeo in 2005, his prospects for programming looked dim. The need for the product the Odeo team had been working on, a podcasting directory, was virtually eliminated when Apple announced that iTunes would contain

WHAT'S WITH BIZ?

Although Stone's passport lists his name as Christopher Isaac Stone, he does not go by that name. Stone told *Marin* magazine in August 2010 that the story behind his name Biz came when he was little and just learning how to talk. He was trying to imitate phonetically how his father, an auto mechanic with a Boston accent, said Christopher.

Stone explained: "To my not-quite-yet-formed ear technology, it sounded very much like "Biz-ah-bah," which was shortened to Biz. I think it was third grade when the information went public. I had a birthday party and my mom said something like, "Okay Biz, time to open presents."[11] The name stuck.

"I don't even answer to Christopher anymore," Stone told *Reuters* in 2009.[12] Stone now asks people to make checks payable to "Isaac Stone." "Sometimes I tell people my name is Isaac when I just don't feel like explaining why my name is Biz. My mother tells people that it's short for Elizabeth."[13] But since his full name is on his passport, Stone says it has led to problems with air travel if his ticket is accidentally booked under "Biz Stone."

a podcasting directory. After locating podcasts using the directory, users could download the podcasts onto Apple iPods. Even before that announcement, Odeo's employees suspected podcasts were not the next big thing. Internet users were not listening to podcasts as much as doing other things online. During this time, Dorsey started taking a fashion class at Apparel Arts, a trade school in San Francisco. He wondered if he should stick with fashion school and design skirts and jeans after all.

A NEW OLD IDEA

Did Odeo simply need a new direction? Williams encouraged Odeo's programmers to brainstorm and come up with new ideas. In Dorsey's opinion, one of the most important characteristics of a successful entrepreneur is the capacity for recognizing opportunities and acting on them. "Cultivate an ability to recognize fortunate situations when they're occurring," he advises.[14]

Much had changed in the online universe between Dorsey's trip to the Bison Paddock in 2000 and Williams's request for ideas in 2005. Social media sites such as MySpace and the newly emerging Facebook had gained acceptance. With

SCREENS GET SMALLER; WORDS DO, TOO

With the advent of texting, or SMS messaging, acronyms such as LOL (laugh out loud), emoticons (pictures or symbols conveying emotion), and other typing shortcuts increased. Twitter's 140-character limit was meant to accommodate texting, making these abbreviations common on the site. Some of the abbreviations that allow users to save space and not write lots of words on tiny screens include: idk (I don't know), smh (shaking my head), brb (be right back), g2g (got to go), l8r (later), and ily (I love you).

the availability of SMS technology in most cellular phones, texting had become an increasingly popular means of communication. People were growing accustomed to sending and receiving short messages on their phones.

Dorsey took his idea for an online real-time SMS off the shelf and asked Williams and others at Odeo if they were interested. They were. +

Williams shows off the Odeo Web site.

Follow your interests

Instant updates from your friends, industry experts, favorite celebrities, and what's happening around the world.

Search Twitter

Twitter encourages users to follow anyone else using the service.

FOLLOW THE LEADER

Dorsey envisioned the service with users following one another in the same way that as a boy he had followed ambulance and police car routes. He never needed permission to do so—no one did. Anyone with a radio scanner could access the emergency calls. Listening in on conversations between drivers and dispatchers keeping track of their activity made Dorsey feel connected to the city. When he first pitched the idea, he wanted to give users that same feeling of being part of a dynamic community. He originally pitched the idea at Odeo as Stat.us. The unusual punctuation is called a domain hack, where a domain other than .com is used in order to have a word as a Web address. In the case of Stat.us, the domain is .us.

A PICNIC IN THE PARK

Dorsey first laid out his idea for Stat.us to coworkers at a San Francisco playground in 2006. He and a few others were eating takeout Mexican food at the park during a hackathon to build programs and applications. Williams had authorized a series of these hackathons, dividing employees into teams whose main purpose was to come up with potential new projects that might rescue Odeo from irrelevance. Sitting on the end of the slide at the playground, Dorsey attempted to sell his coworkers on building a real-time SMS. The idea was simple and straightforward. Why wouldn't it succeed? he reasoned. Why wouldn't

people want an easy way to keep in touch
with friends?

Glass, one of the team members who eventually
helped create the prototype for Twitter, says it took
him a while to understand Dorsey's excitement. Once
he did, he was hooked. "There was a moment when
I was sitting with Jack and I said, 'Oh, I do see how
this could really come together to make something
really compelling.'"[1] The more they worked on the
project, the more Glass's enthusiasm grew.

WHAT'S IN A NAME?

Dorsey, Glass, and their team still had not come up
with the perfect name for the service. They needed
something better than Stat.us that still spoke to what
the product was all about.

Dorsey preferred a name that conveyed
movement. They considered Jitter and Twitch.
Twitch seemed almost right as cell phones twitch
and buzz when receiving messages, but the word
also conjured up negative images associated with
twitching or being twitchy. Finally, Glass turned to
the New Oxford English Dictionary. He scanned
the long list of words beginning with the letters
tw and found *twitter*. He and his team agreed to

Stone brought his blogging expertise to the Twitter project.

take out the vowels, inspired by Web sites such as
Flickr and Tumblr. Twttr was also five characters,
the length of SMS codes in the United States. SMS
codes are special numbers shorter than full telephone

WHY 140 CHARACTERS?

When Dorsey and his team built the Twitter program, they assumed most users would post updates on their phones. An SMS text message has a 160-character limit. Messages longer than 160 characters are divided into multiple texts. Today, most cell phone customers pay a flat fee for unlimited texting. But in 2006, the majority of customers paid per text. To help prevent Twitter users from racking up large phone bills, engineers limited tweets to 140 characters, which allowed 20 extra characters for a user name and colon in front of the update.

numbers that are used to send SMS messages. They are meant to be easier to read and remember than regular telephone numbers.

Stone was one of the programmers who worked on the Twttr prototype. He loved blogging, and, out of everyone at Odeo, seemed primed to share Dorsey's faith in the viability of an online message service. Today, tweeting is sometimes referred to as microblogging because it allows users to express themselves, like a blog does, but they do so in posts that can be no longer than 140 characters.

In February 2006, Stone, Glass, Dorsey, and their team unveiled to their fellow employees Twttr, a system by which a text message could be sent to one SMS number and users could receive that message on their phones as a text. Most people used standard cell phones to text. Twttr provided a code, 40404, for users to text messages to the service via their phones. Messages could also be posted on twttr.com, which included an option for mobile phone delivery. It did not wow everyone at the meeting, but it did persuade Williams to allow them to keep going.

"A DISASTER IN THE MAKING"

When Odeo officially launched Twttr in July 2006, the online magazine *TechCrunch* gave it a review. Michael Arrington, the reviewer, basically liked the service, but he had a few reservations about it. This included whether users would balk at the lack of privacy involved in posting

A FORGOTTEN FOUNDER?

"It was right there on my desk. I could just pick it up and take it anywhere in the world. That was a really fun time," recalled Glass.[2] At that time, the entire service ran off of his IBM ThinkPad computer. Many inside the company remember Glass as a crucial advocate for the Twitter project and claim it wouldn't exist without him. So why is the official roster of cofounders a trio—Williams, Stone, and Dorsey—instead of a quartet? Why was Glass's name left off the list?

Not long after Williams bought Odeo back from its investors, he fired Glass. Supporters of Glass have suggested a couple of theories. Some say it was a matter of conflicting personalities. Williams was quiet and Glass was loud, and the two men did not work well together. Others wonder if Williams felt threatened by Glass who seemed interested in running the company. Whatever the case, Glass stresses the collaborative nature of Twitter's development and says other employees also have gone without credit. "The reality is it was a group effort," he says. "It came out of conversations."[3]

messages that all could see. He also questioned the wisdom of Odeo's dabbling in side projects when "their primary product line [podcasting service] is, besides the excellent design, a total snoozer."[4] Reader comments on Arrington's article showed that other people found the service less than promising. "Not innovative and not focused," said one critic and followed with the prediction, "Twttr sounds like a disaster in the making." A particularly scathing remark read, "Glad to see I'm not the only one who thinks Odeo is O-dead-o."[5]

In a way, that commenter was right. Odeo did not have long to live. The investors who had signed on to fund a podcasting company suddenly found themselves involved with a business venture that seemed headed in an uncertain direction—or maybe no direction at all. Who knew what Odeo's future would bring?

AN OBVIOUS SOLUTION

Six months after Twttr was unveiled to Odeo employees, Twttr changed to Twitter. As CEO, Williams offered to buy back the company from its investors in September 2006. In the letter outlining his proposal, Williams apologized for Odeo's failings and mentioned Twitter as "one of the pieces of value that I see in Odeo, but it's much too early to tell what's there."[6] He said he "would continue to invest in Twitter," but he understood why others on the board might not want to back the venture, "especially since [their initial investment] was for a different market altogether."[7]

That same month, while making an appearance at a computer industry conference in San Francisco, Williams spoke honestly about mistakes he had made at Odeo. One key problem, he said, was "not building for people like ourselves."[8] Odeo was a podcasting company. Yet no one who worked there listened to podcasts very often or found them especially interesting. In general, Williams said, he was guilty of "not listening to my gut" and trying too hard to please investors while

VENTURE CAPITAL

Rarely is a start-up company funded by a single investor. Usually, it takes a lot of money, or capital, to get a start-up up and running. Entrepreneurs seek assistance not only from wealthy individuals but also from venture capital firms. These are companies that exist specifically to invest in fledgling businesses and make a profit when those businesses prosper. Glass launched Odeo Corporation with the help of about a dozen investors, including Williams and the venture capital firm Charles River Ventures.

ignoring his instincts about what path Odeo should take.[9]

The investors agreed to sell their shares in the company to Williams. From Odeo's ashes, he created a new start-up: Obvious Corporation. With Obvious, he planned to stick by his preferred business model of keeping things small, experimental, and devoted to projects like Twitter—projects he and his fellow employees truly cared about. Dorsey, Stone, and other Odeo veterans made the switch to Obvious. Williams appointed Stone to be the new company's creative director and gave Dorsey the job of CEO. Having never held a management position before, Dorsey was nervous. But he was the one with the creative vision for Twitter, thus Williams felt he deserved a chance to take control. Dorsey removed his nose ring and began dressing more formally in an attempt to look the part of a business executive.

Writing about the buyout on his personal blog, Williams conveyed a sense of optimism. "I believe there is a lot of value in what we've built—both Odeo and Twitter. . . . In the new company, with a new structure, and a new model, I believe they are great investments."[10]

HOW TWITTER WORKS

On Facebook, in order to friend someone, that person must accept the friend request. The Web site requires all relationships to be mutual. Users cannot access other users' profiles unless both parties agree or if one of the users selects settings that allows his or her profile to be publicly visible. Facebook users can acquire thousands of friends, but depending on their privacy settings, the information they share stays within that select group.

Twitter works differently. You can follow someone on your Twitter feed, and that person does not have to follow you in return. Pop star Lady Gaga has approximately 16 million followers, none of whom first needed her permission to view her posts.

Glass said being able to go online and read a brief synopsis of

A CREATIVE INTERVIEW

Well-known *New York Times* columnist Maureen Dowd was skeptical of Twitter's usefulness and not afraid to be cranky about it. She interviewed Williams and Stone for the paper in 2009 and required them to limit their responses to 140 characters. The results are amusing. The following excerpt is from the interview, headlined "To Tweet or Not to Tweet":

MD: "Did you know you were designing a toy for bored celebrities and high-school girls?"

BS: "We definitely didn't design it for that. If they want to use it for that, it's great."

MD: "Do you ever think 'I don't care if my friend is having a hamburger?'"

BS: "If I said I was eating a hamburger, Evan would be surprised because I'm a vegan."[11]

what a friend is doing or thinking at a given moment "makes you feel like you're right with that person. It's a whole emotional impact."[12]

There is a term for the feeling Glass described: ambient awareness or ambient intimacy. Technology writer Stephen Johnson, in an article for *Time* magazine, defined ambient awareness as the "strangely satisfying glimpse" into other people's daily routines that Twitter and other social network sites offer.[13] With Twitter, Johnson pointed out, you can feel equally connected to family members, friends you have known for decades, or celebrities you have never met. For example, Johnson said, "You glance at your Twitter feed over that first cup of coffee, and in a few seconds you find out that your nephew got into med school and Shaquille O'Neal just finished a cardio workout in Phoenix."[14]

Twitter's creators designed it to be used on mobile phones.

Apple launched the iPhone in June 2007, making it
even easier for people to use Twitter.

ENCOURAGING SIGNS AND GROWING PAINS

n March of every year, innovators in the fields
of music, film, and technology converge in
Austin, Texas, for South by Southwest (SXSW),
one of the largest and liveliest multimedia festivals
in the country. Attendees can see performances

by up-and-coming bands, watch cutting-edge independent movies, and get the latest news on technological advances.

At 2007 SXSW Interactive, the technology portion of the festival, the buzz was all about Twitter. Its presence was hard to miss. Obvious strategically placed two large plasma screens by the conference registration desk. A continuous stream of tweets appeared on the screens that gave conference-goers the inside scoop on what was happening at the festival, including which panel discussions were hot and where to find the best parties at night. Obvious also positioned a screen in a hallway where attendees gathered after presentations. Before long, everyone was swamping the screens or checking their phones to find out what Twitter users had to say. At the height of the festival, the volume of tweets-per-day ballooned from 20,000 to 60,000. Obvious returned to San Francisco with an award for Twitter in the Blog category.

SHAKING THINGS UP

In Austin, Dorsey, Williams, and the Obvious team saw firsthand how well Twitter worked for coordinating social events. Several months earlier,

EMERGENCY SERVICE

Victims of major natural disasters have used Twitter to update family, friends, and the wider world about their situation, beginning with the San Francisco earthquake in 2006. Other disasters included the earthquakes in Haiti on January 12, 2010, and in Japan on March 11, 2011. Users posted photos of the devastation, provided updates on rescue operations, and communicated valuable information to survivors on the state of relief services.

Following the earthquake in Haiti, Twitter user Frederic Dupoux tweeted: "everybody camping in the streets of port-au-prince sleeping under stars to wake up from an awful nightmare." Partners in Health, a Boston-based organization, tweeted: "We are mobilizing resources and preparing plans to bring medical assistance to areas that have been hardest hit."[2]

in August 2006, they had gotten a glimpse of a potential use for their new product. On August 3, a small earthquake hit the San Francisco Bay Area. Twitter users—of which there were only a few thousand at the time—felt the tremors and reached for their phones to broadcast the news. As the online magazine *Business Insider* later reported in an article on Twitter milestones, "It might have been the first time people realized Twitter might be good for something more than saying what kind of sandwich was for lunch."[1]

Still, even after Twitter's success at SXSW, critics predicted the service would never amount to much. In April 2007, Twitter had approximately 80,000 users. That month, *BusinessWeek* highlighted the debate being waged among bloggers who wondered "whether Twitter represent[ed] a leap forward in online communication or the first, faint chirps of an attention apocalypse."[3] Was Twitter just another mark of our increasingly fragmented and distracted lives? Had we become so unable to focus that we could only absorb information if it was delivered in tiny blips and blurts? Perhaps it was "creepy," as the article said one blogger wrote, to be "constantly connected."[4]

FAIL WHALE

Creepy or not, Twitter was growing quickly. Apple had released the iPhone in June 2007, and this instantly popular device made it even easier for Twitter users to access the service. Skyrocketing traffic on the site put a strain on the software. Dorsey and the Obvious computer engineers had trouble updating the technology quickly enough to keep pace with demand. "It just got a lot bigger a lot faster than expected," Williams later reflected.[5] Unfortunately, Twitter users became accustomed to logging on to their accounts and seeing the Fail Whale, a cartoon image of a whale being lifted from the ocean via a rope net held aloft by a flock of birds. This was accompanied by an error message: "Twitter is over capacity. Too many tweets! Please wait a moment and try again."[6]

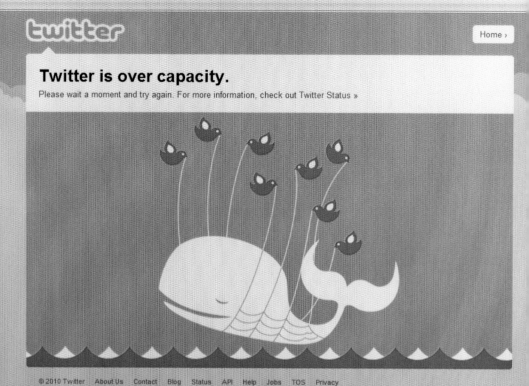

Yiying Lu's illustration has become one of the most iconic
images associated with Twitter.

As Twitter took flight, strain within the
company rose as well. Dorsey was overwhelmed
with juggling the duties of programmer and CEO.
Admittedly, he never felt entirely comfortable
in the latter role. Years later, in the *Vanity Fair*
magazine interview, he analyzed his time as CEO
and explained why the job was never really a good fit
for him:

I let myself be in a weird position because it always felt like Ev's company. . . . I was this new guy who was a programmer, who had a good idea. I would not be strong in my convictions, basically, because he was the older, wiser one.[7]

A SHIFT IN THE RANKS

Eventually, the "older, wiser one" regained control. By April 2007, Twitter had separated from Obvious Corporation to become its own entity—Twitter Inc. Williams had spent much of his time working on other Obvious projects and let Dorsey run the show. In 2008, with Twitter's popularity exploding, Williams decided to realign his priorities. In October, he proposed to the board of directors that he take over as CEO. Dorsey would stay connected to the company as board chairman, but his day-to-day presence in the office would cease. Even though Dorsey knew Williams had more

THE ORIGIN OF THE FAIL WHALE

Yiying Lu, a Chinese graphic designer living in Australia, created the now infamous image. Artists post work that they allow others to use for free on iStockPhoto.com. Twitter found the picture on the site and liked its representation of team effort. Lu, however, had a different reason for making the sea creature carried by birds. She said, "It was initially created as a birthday e-card for an overseas friend of mine when I was in my last year study at University—expressing my: Sorry I am failed to be there across the ocean, but here is a little console from my heart."[8]

TWITTER LINGO

In addition to *tweet* and *Fail Whale*, a host of other terms are unique to Twitter, some coined by users.

· Hashtag: Twitter users came up with a method of categorizing related posts by topic. If a message is about the Super Bowl, for instance, a poster can tag it with the # symbol followed by superbowl (e.g., #superbowl). Anyone looking for information on the Super Bowl can do a Twitter search and find all posts marked with that hashtag.

· Retweet: Messages spread like wildfire with retweets. Someone writes a tweet, and someone else who finds the tweet interesting passes it on by retweeting it, sometimes with additional comments. Messages travel along the chain from one Twitter user to another.

· @messages: When the @ symbol is placed before an account name (e.g., @jack), it designates the message as being directed to or about a particular person. It is a way to hold more personal conversations within the larger system.

· Tweetup: Sometimes, Twitter users want to get together offline. A tweetup notice can be posted to invite users with common interests—from orchid growers to legal scholars—to a face-to-face gathering.

business experience than he did and would likely do a better job in the position, he took the transition hard. "It was like being punched in the stomach," he said.[9] Stone viewed the situation in practical terms: "We had two very strong leaders here, and we really needed to choose one."[10]

RIDING THE ROCKET

Even a strong leader such as Williams, with more than 6 million registrations and $20 million contributed by investors, could not really keep ahead of Twitter's incredible success. The Fail Whale continued rising into the sky as the company reported an increase to 6 million users by the end of 2008. That fall, Facebook offered to buy Twitter for a reported price of $500 million of Facebook stock. Williams and the board turned down the deal. Though Twitter essentially had no revenue yet—it did not sell ads or charge users for any aspect of service—the feeling was that its value and influence would only increase. It had grown so much in such a short time. Who could predict how much farther it would go? "We were just hanging on by our fingernails to a rocket ship," Williams told a reporter for the *New York Times* in 2010.[11]

As 2008 drew to a close, even US president-elect Barack Obama had hopped aboard the Twitter rocket. In the early morning hours of November 3, the day after the presidential election, Obama's

HOW DOES TWITTER MAKE MONEY?

In the beginning, Twitter did not make money. Dorsey has said the company values user experience first. Their early goal was to expand the service and attract subscribers more than to generate income. Since then, Twitter has started selling ads in the form of promoted tweets, promoted trends, and promoted accounts. While a tweet from an advertiser is clearly marked as such, it is embedded within followers' feeds. This allows the users to find out, for example, about a special on lattes at Starbucks in the same form they find out about their cousin's new baby. It is all part of the company's plan to have ads that are informative but unobtrusive.

Twitter followers received this thank-you tweet: "We just made history. All of this happened because you gave your time, talent, and passion. All of this happened because of you."[12]

By December 2008, Twitter had exploded. There were 3 million registered users on Twitter, including politicians, movie stars, and famous athletes such as NBA legend Shaquille O'Neal and champion biker Lance Armstrong. Companies such as Starbucks and Whole Foods suddenly found an exciting, new way to promote their products to customers. Everyone, it seemed, was using Twitter. +

President Obama's campaign effectively used Twitter in 2008.

Twitter's founders at the *Time* 100 gala

TWEET, TWEET
LITTLE STAR

*T*ime magazine announced its annual *Time* 100 list in April 2009 to recognize "the people who most affect our world."[1] The Twitter founders—Williams, Stone, and Dorsey—were number one in the Builders and Titans category.

Although only Williams and Stone were pictured, the magazine explicitly honored all three men. The accompanying short article describing their accomplishments was written by film and television star Ashton Kutcher—perhaps their biggest fan. Not only had Twitter made celebrities of its founders, it became a venue for celebrities such as Kutcher, talk show host Ellen DeGeneres, and pop star Britney Spears to candidly share their thoughts, feelings, and opinions with those who were interested.

CONNECTING WITH FANS

Kutcher was an early and prolific Twitter user and one of the first users to attract more than 1 million followers. He had a contest with CNN News to see who could reach that number first, and he won. He compared Williams, Stone, and Dorsey to telephone inventor Alexander Graham Bell and other pioneers in communications technology. He also explained

RIP JON BON JOVI?

In December 2011, rocker Jon Bon Jovi became the subject of a Twitter death hoax. A fan from Pennsylvania started the rumor of Bon Jovi's demise on a friend's Twitter account. He later claimed he did it because he was frustrated by the singer's dearth of musical output in recent years. To counter the heavily retweeted message, Bon Jovi posted a photo of himself holding a homemade sign reading "Heaven looks a lot like New Jersey, December 19th, 2011" on his Twitter and Facebook pages.

STARS AT THE TOP

As of December 2011, the top ten most followed celebrities on Twitter were:

1. Lady Gaga (@ladygaga, 16,425,213)
2. Justin Bieber (@justinbieber, 14,901,452)
3. Katy Perry (@katyperry, 12,491,526)
4. Kim Kardashian (@kimkardashian, 11,563,052)
5. Britney Spears (@britneyspears, 11,388,800)
6. Barack Obama (@barackobama, 11,326,837)
7. Shakira (@shakira, 10,802,237)
8. Rihanna (@rihanna, 10,073,974)
9. Taylor Swift (@taylorswift13, 9,457,443)
10. Selena Gomez (@selenagomez, 8,603,871)

how the service had expanded his horizons. "For someone like me who lives in a construct of filtered communication—packaged and polished by the industry that employees me—Twitter has become a new industry for expressing myself and accessing cultural trends, opinions, and information."[2] Now, he could communicate with fans directly, and they could get to know him in a more personal manner than a brief television interview or tabloid news flash allowed.

In a way, celebrities had become like the ambulances Dorsey tracked through the streets of Saint Louis as a child. People could follow them and feel as if they were hitching a ride into the world of the rich and famous. What's more, followers potentially have an impact on their idols' lives. If Lady Gaga tweeted that she was looking for a good pancake recipe,

As of 2011, Lady Gaga was the most followed celebrity on Twitter.

any of her nearly 20 million followers could respond. What fraction, if any, of those responses she or her staff would actually read is unknown. But followers at least had the satisfaction of imagining the pop star sitting down at the breakfast table to a plate of raspberry-chocolate chip-hazelnut flapjacks from their own recipe.

CHARITY AND SELF-PROMOTION

On a less superficial level, celebrities have used Twitter feeds to increase awareness of their favorite charitable causes. Kutcher has kept his followers informed about the nonprofit organization Malaria No More, which is dedicated to wiping out the malaria virus in Africa. Twitter users can embed links to articles and Web sites within their posts that point followers toward more in-depth information published elsewhere online. As Kutcher said in a *Time* magazine article, his 140-character messages can encourage readers to learn about "the causes close to my heart."[3]

Twitter is also a promotional tool recording artists can use to publicize their new music and movie stars can use to promote their new movies. Basketball legend Shaquille O'Neal, another early celebrity on Twitter, had a thread on his feed named "Random Acts of Shaqness." He made a contest out of encouraging fans to meet up with him before

Ashton Kutcher was an early and enthusiastic user of Twitter.

games so he could give them complimentary tickets. O'Neal would post tweets such as, "People n phoenix u have 5 min to touch me I have 2 laker tickets n my hand I'm on a corner at a bus stop."[4] The giveaways emphasized his image as a nice, approachable guy and attracted followers to his feed.

TWITTER: FRIEND OR FOE OF LITERACY?

Not every celebrity is enamored of Twitter. British actor Ralph Fiennes blames Twitter and other social media sites for the dumbing down of language. Speaking at a British film industry festival, Fiennes said,

Our expressiveness and our ease with some words is being diluted so that the sentence with more than one clause is a problem for us, and the word of more than two syllables is a problem for us.[5]

Yet his opinions are at odds with those of celebrated literary figure Margaret Atwood. The Canadian novelist and poet believes Twitter encourages a love of reading and writing. As she says,

People have to actually be able to read and write to use the Internet, so it's a great literacy driver if kids are given the tools and the incentive to learn the skills that allow them to access it.[6]

Atwood has more than 7,000 followers on Twitter. She compares the tweet to other historically short forms of writing, including the telegraph and the smoke signal. "It's like carving your name on a tree."[7]

CELEBRATED FAKES

Couldn't anyone register as Beyoncé or Justin Bieber and start sending tweets under that name? Twitter took measures to prevent becoming a breeding ground for celebrity impostors. In 2009, Twitter launched a verification service for its high-profile subscribers. A verified account would display a special seal to reassure followers of the account's authenticity.

Still, determined fakers can always find ways to circumvent the rules, and, in one highly publicized instance, the celebrity impersonated did not mind.

@MAYOREMANUEL

In 2010, Journalism professor Dan Sinker created the hilarious fake account @MayorEmanuel to poke fun at the Chicago Democratic mayoral candidate and former White House Chief of Staff Rahm Emanuel. The account had legions of devoted followers— including the real Emanuel! Sinker managed to keep his own identity a secret through 1,942 tweets in which he pretended to document the campaign of the notoriously potty-mouthed candidate. As the story progressed, Sinker-as-Rahm's adventures grew wackier and wackier, making it obvious the account was not real. Supporting characters in the saga included a dog named Hambone and Quaxelrod, a duck with a moustache. Yet followers continued to read @MayorEmanual's every tweet. It was as though they were reading a gripping novel, which, in a sense, they were. After Sinker's identity became known, the real Mayor Emanuel donated $5,000 to Sinker's favorite charity, Young Chicago Authors, as a no-hard-feelings gesture.

EVERYONE CAN BE A STAR

Some people tweet because they are famous; some people tweet so often that they become famous. One breed of "Twilebrity" amasses followers by dedicating their lives to online communicating. Freelance journalist Stefanie Michaels, who has gained more than 1 million followers through sheer volume of correspondence by tweeting, says, ". . . more than all of the [Twitter] founders combined."[9] Twitter, however, suspends accounts of subscribers who post more than 1,000 tweets per day.

Although @MayorEmanuel was a piece of fiction, Alexis Madrigal wrote about Sinker's hoax in the *Atlantic* magazine. He noted that @MayorEmanuel had a vitality that most fiction does not share because the story was happening in real time, referencing real events, albeit from a made-up perspective:

> *The character could be right there with you when the Bears (or the Democrats) lost or when snow blew in or as Rahm visited Google. [Sinker] created fiction both out of what was happening and out of what you, yourself, were living. And he did it for five months. It was serialization in a sense, but alive.*[8]

If a fictional, "real-time" news story could be this captivating, imagine how engrossing the news could be when it was real. +

The fake Twitter account for Chicago mayoral candidate Rahm Emanuel had 37,650 followers by the time it reached its final tweet.

Twitter user Sohaib Athar unknowingly live-tweeted the raid on Osama bin Laden.

LIVE-TWEETING HISTORY

Sohaib Athar, a Pakistani information technology consultant, had moved to Abbottabad in northeast Pakistan to get away from the crowds and noise in Lahore, Pakistan. He was less than thrilled to hear the roar of a helicopter

flying over his house at 1:00 a.m. on May 2, 2011.
"Go away helicopter—before I take out my
giant swatter :-/," he tweeted under his handle
@ReallyVirtual.[1]

Instead of putting a pillow over his head and
going back to sleep, Athar stayed on Twitter and
tried to figure out what was going on. He gathered
details from other Twitter users who were also
awakened by the atypical racket. At one point, he
shared: "@mohcin the few people online at this
time of night are saying one of the copters was not
Pakistani . . ."[2]

For hours, Athar and his online companions
traded observations about the reported bomb
blasts, the news of a helicopter crashing in the area,
and the police beginning door-to-door searches.
One subscriber suggested a possible connection
between the events unfolding in Abbottabad and a
forthcoming address by President Obama that was
suddenly announced on Twitter just five hours after
Athar first broadcast news of the disturbance. At
10:00 a.m. in Pakistan, @ReallyVirtual posted this
revelation: "Uh oh, now I'm the guy who liveblogged
the Osama raid without knowing it."[3]

President Obama's speech, given around
midnight eastern standard time, confirmed the

death of Osama bin Laden. The notorious leader of the international terrorist network al-Qaeda had been on the run since masterminding the September 11, 2001, terrorist attacks on the United States. During the surprise attack, led by the United States, on bin Laden's secret Abbottabad compound, Navy SEALS landed two helicopters, stormed into the residence, and killed bin Laden.

Word of bin Laden's death soon escalated on Twitter. At 3,000 tweets per second, it set a new record. Athar's tweet about the helicopter started the unprecedented flurry of messages. He was right there, covering events as they happened.

ATHAR REPORTS

Sohaib Athar posted the following tweets chronicling the bin Laden raid in real time:

A huge window shaking bang here in Abbottabad Cantt. I hope its not the start of something nasty :-S

Since taliban (probably) don't have helicpoters [sic], and since they're saying it was not "ours", so must be a complicated situation #abbottabad

The abbottabad helicopter/UFO was shot down near the Bilal Town area, and there's report of a flash. People saying it could be a drone.

Report from a taxi driver: The army has cordoned off the crash area and is conducting door-to-door search in the surrounding.

RT: Osama Bin Laden killed in Abbottabad, Pakistan.: ISI has confirmed it << Uh oh, there goes the neighborhood :-/[4]

TWITTER REVOLUTIONS

Across the globe, Twitter is not only a venue for reporting news, but it has become a tool for making news happen. At various times, the recent political uprisings in the countries of Iran, Moldova, Tunisia, and Egypt have been dubbed "Twitter Revolutions" by the media. Protestors reportedly used Twitter, Facebook, and other social media sites to organize protests. The high speed and vast range of electronically spread messages mean crowds can assemble quickly in numbers too massive to be controlled.

In some countries, government leaders have ordered shutdowns of Internet and mobile phone service in an attempt to thwart protestors. In January 2011, Egypt's President Hosni Mubarak did just that. It was his means of combatting the thousands of protestors mobbing Cairo's Tahrir Square who demanded his

THE ARAB SPRING

The Arab Spring is the name given to a wave of political uprisings in Arab countries. It began with a Tunisian street vendor, Mohamed Bouazizi, who set himself on fire in December 2010 as an act of political protest. A month later, pressured by street demonstrations arising in support of Bouazizi, Tunisia's president, Zine al-Abidine Ben Ali, ended his 23-year rule and fled the country. Since then, revolutions have broken out in Egypt, Libya, Yemen, Bahrain, Algeria, and other countries. Some observers have argued that social media has played a vital part in organizing this ongoing revolutionary age.

Protestors in Egypt reportedly used Twitter to coordinate their demonstrations.

resignation. The shutdown did not last long, and Mubarak was forced from office just a few weeks later. Mubarak's resignation topped the list of Twitter's most tweeted stories of 2011.

MUCH ADO ABOUT NOTHING?

Critics have argued that Twitter's role in Egypt and elsewhere has been overstated. Although Twitter and

Facebook may have gotten the word out to some Egyptians, the majority of the country, according to Anne Applebaum in the *Washington Post*, did not have Internet access:

> For all the guff being spoken about Twitter and social media, the uprising in Cairo appears to be a very old-fashioned, almost 19th-century revolution: People see other people going out in the streets and decide to join them.[5]

What Twitter unarguably did, however, was spread news of Egypt's revolution and others like it throughout the wider world. Links to video footage of atrocities such as riot police shooting and beating protestors were tweeted and retweeted. In countries such as Iran, Twitter has become a vital way to circumvent government control of traditional media. Iranian leaders have the power to censor stories reported on television and in the papers, but they cannot effectively prevent

WHAT'S THE BUZZ?

Twitter engineers developed a computer algorithm to identify topics that are being tweeted at that very second. Called "trending topics," they appear in a list on the Twitter home page. Users sometimes add a hashtag to identify the subject so others can find it in a search or use it in their own tweets. Individual users can adjust the settings so the trending topic list on their page either shows popular worldwide topics or those in their geographic area.

ordinary citizens from tweeting the news on their phones.

A CROWD THAT CANNOT BE DISPERSED

In 2009, Iran's citizens took to the streets of Tehran, Iran's capital city, to protest presidential election results they believed were rigged. Writing on the one-year anniversary of what became known as Iran's 2009 Green Revolution, political columnist Charles Krauthammer observed, "Twitter cannot stop a bullet."[6] But it can let the world know bullets have been fired. It can sound the alarm for injustice and convince sympathizers to join forces, wherever they are, to fight against oppressive regimes.

"A crowd that's always connected," wrote Bill Wasik in *Wired* magazine, "can never really be dispersed. It's always still out there."[7] As more and more people in more and more countries gain Internet access, the strength of their numbers grows. As Wasik points out,

> *For tech to become effective as a tool for civic disorder, it first had to insinuate itself into people's daily lives. Now that it has there can be no getting rid of it. The agent provocateur lies inside our pockets and purses and cannot be uninstalled.*[8]

Egyptian protestors drew the logos of
social networks on their encampment.

Evan Williams, seen here with his wife, Sarah,
stepped down as CEO of Twitter in 2011.

THE FUTURE OF TWITTER

After three years away from Twitter, Dorsey returned in the role of executive chairman in March 2011. Things had changed in the three years while Dorsey was exploring new ventures, including a new start-up called Square. Twitter now had 250 employees and had evolved from a social media site where users simply broadcast thoughts and feelings, into what Dorsey and his colleagues now regularly called an "information network."[1]

The company also had a new CEO, Dick Costolo, to replace Williams after he decided to step down from the position. On March 29, 2011, Williams posted a message on his personal blog, Evhead, titled "An Obvious Next Step." After five years at Twitter, two of those years as CEO, he had become restless and wanted to explain why. Among other things, he wrote,

> *The reason I left Blogger/Google when I did is that I felt it had reached a place where it was on solid ground and in capable hands . . . Though still an independent company, I realized Twitter may be at a similar*

HIP TO BE SQUARE

During the three years Dorsey was away from Twitter, he launched a new start-up in May 2010 called Square Inc. with his friend Jim McKelvey. The company developed a way to turn smartphones into credit card readers with a tiny, white magnetic card reader in the shape of a square. The card reader attaches to the headphone jack of an iPhone, iPad, or Android device. Merchants who subscribe to Square obtained this hardware for free, but paid 2.75 percent of each transaction process. A merchant swipes the customer's credit card through the card reader attached to his or her mobile device, enters the amount to be paid, and receives payment the next day as a direct deposit into his or her bank account. A text-messaged receipt is sent to the customer, and no paper ever changes hands.

point today. So, as was reported in various places yesterday, I've decided to scale back my role at the company. I'm still involved, but it's no longer my full-time job.[2]

Williams did not say anything definite about his future plans, but the title of his blog post held a clue. In June 2011, Stone also stepped away from Twitter and joined Williams in taking that "Obvious Next Step." Together with Jason Goldman, a mutual friend from their Google days, they relaunched Twitter's birthplace— Obvious Corporation. The mission statement they crafted revealed their optimism for what it could accomplish: "The Obvious Corporation develops systems that help people work together to improve the world."[3] Maybe they did not know yet what those systems would be—or maybe they did but were not ready to reveal them—but their shared history at Twitter taught them to aim high.

BIGGER AND BETTER

In a blog post of his own, Stone reflected on Twitter's early days, when only he and the other cofounders sustained faith in its worth:

> *It was something we were endlessly ridiculed for as being 'useless' but we believed in it and Evan believed in us so he kept funding us until Twitter started spreading like wildfire.*[5]

And Williams, in his March 29 farewell, demonstrated his

CONSOLIDATE POWER

Dick Costolo was known for his quick thinking long before he became Twitter's Chief Operations Officer (COO) in September 2009, and eventually CEO in 2011. After college, he joined an improvisational theater troupe in Chicago. One of the troupe's comedy bits was to have the audience call out absurd scientific hypotheses, such as the moon is actually a giant marshmallow or George Washington had toads living under his toenails. Costolo and the other actors had to respond with equally crazy evidence to support the hypotheses. He left improv in 1994 to launch a string of Internet companies, including Feedburner, which he sold to Google in 2007. Through it all, he kept his sharp wit.

On his first day as Twitter COO, he joked in a tweet: "First full day as Twitter COO tomorrow. Task #1: undermine CEO, consolidate power."[6] He took on the role of CEO temporarily when Williams went on leave. His position became permanent when Williams decided to step down. Costolo has been instrumental in the formulation of ad campaigns and other revenue-boosting plans at Twitter.

A PRINCELY SUM

In December 2011, Saudi Arabian Prince Alwaleed bin Talal Abdulaziz Alsaud, one of the richest men in the world, invested $300 million in Twitter, making it the largest investment from a single individual the company has ever received. Observers found it ironic that a member of Middle Eastern royalty would back a Web site credited with helping facilitate the Arab Spring political uprising. But Alwaleed praised the service for having a global impact.

continued faith, saying, "I will venture a prediction about what's next for Twitter: It will be bigger and better."[7]

How big had Twitter become? By the middle of 2011, the company announced its 100 million active users out of 175 million registered users worldwide were sending 200 million tweets a day. Twitter's official blog offered a mind-boggling illustration of the tweet-per-day statistic, saying it equaled "a 10-million page book in tweets or 8,163 copies of Leo Tolstoy's *War and Peace*."[8] Twitter was also scheduled to integrate later that year with the new Apple operating system. That meant it would automatically be part of any iPhone, iPad, or iPod. The theoretical stack of Tolstoy's novel seemed destined to reach the moon.

Stone used an analogy from biology instead of literature to

Dorsey split his time between Square and Twitter as of March 2012.

convey Twitter's power. He compared it to a multi-celled organism in which single cells "join forces" to create something greater than themselves. "Twitter allows people all over the world to join forces and make amazing things happen," he wrote on his blog.[9]

Twitter's new headquarters in San Francisco

CREATING AN AMAZING FUTURE

Now it was Dorsey and Costolo's challenge to manage Twitter and ensure that amazing things kept happening. On December 8, 2011, the company unveiled a major redesign of the site, uncluttering the layout with the intent of making the site easier and faster to use. Speaking from their future new headquarters in a historic San Francisco building undergoing renovation, Dorsey said, "Twitter should be equally accessible for those who know the shortcuts and for those who don't."[10] He realized that new subscribers sometimes found the site confusing, visiting once or twice and never coming back. With the new design, which they were calling Fly, Twitter engineers strove to eliminate potential sources of frustration.

Among the new features was the Discover tab, which readers could click on to locate topics of interest. This tab marked Twitter's shifting view of itself from a social network to an information network. "When you use Discover, you'll see results reflecting your interests based on your current location, what you follow, and what's happening in the world,"[11] proclaimed the company Web site. Twitter was now the primary news source for many of its subscribers. Dorsey wanted to help people find what they wanted to find when they wanted to find it.

TWITTER'S NEW DIGS

To renew their commitment to staying in San Francisco and make room for their expanding staff, Twitter planned to move to new headquarters in 2012. The building they chose at 1355 Market Street was built in 1937 and had been the site of a wholesale furniture market. The company renovated the building, which had been empty for years and needed a complete remodeling. It was part of a larger effort to help revitalize the surrounding neighborhood.

According to company spokeswoman Jodi Olson, the aim was for "Twitter to be approachable for every single person on the planet."[12] At the rate Twitter has grown and is still growing, it does not seem like such an unreachable goal. +

Twitter CEO Dick Costolo in 2011

TIMELINE

1972	1974	1976
Evan Williams is born on March 31, near Clarks, Nebraska.	Christopher Isaac "Biz" Stone is born on March 10, in Wellesley, Massachusetts.	Jack Dorsey is born in Saint Louis, Missouri, on November 19.

2000	2000	2004
Dorsey sends his test message from the Bison Paddock at Golden Gate Park in July.	Stone and Marc Ginsburg launch Xanga.com.	Williams leaves Google and cofounds Odeo, a podcasting company, with Noah Glass. Stone joins them at Odeo.

1997

Dorsey moves to New York City, attends NYU, and works as a programmer for DMS, a courier dispatch company.

1998

Dorsey and his business partner, Greg Kidd, move to San Francisco to launch an online dispatch service.

1999

Pyra Labs, cofounded by Williams, launches Blogger.

2005

Dorsey is hired to work at Odeo.

2006

Dorsey sends the first tweet—"just setting up my twttr"—in March.

2006

Odeo launches Twttr in July, which becomes Twitter in the fall.

TIMELINE

2006	2007	2007
Williams, Stone, Dorsey, and other former Odeo employees found Obvious Corporation. Dorsey becomes CEO.	Apple releases the iPhone in June, increasing Twitter's accessibility.	Twitter is a hit at the South by Southwest (SXSW) media festival in Austin, Texas, in March.

2009	2011	2011
Iran's Green Revolution protesting presidential election results is dubbed a "Twitter Revolution" in the media.	Williams steps down as Twitter's CEO. Dick Costolo takes over the job.	Dorsey returns to Twitter.

2008

Twitter grows too fast for the company to keep up, and the site frequently crashes.

2009

New York ferry rider Janis Krums tweets the first photo of US Airways Flight 1549 downed in the Hudson River.

2009

Celebrity Ashton Kutcher becomes the first Twitter user to reach 1 million followers in April.

2011

At midyear, Twitter reports 200 million tweets per day.

2011

Twitter unveils Fly, which is a redesign of its Web site to make the service simpler to use.

ESSENTIAL FACTS

CREATORS

Jack Dorsey (November 19, 1976–)

Christopher "Biz" Stone (March 10, 1974–)

Evan Williams (March 31, 1972–)

Employees at Odeo Corporation

DATE LAUNCHED

July 2006

CHALLENGES

When Twitter was first launched, many thought Jack Dorsey's vision of an online real-time short message service would add up to trivial information on the Internet. The service quickly took off—too fast for the company to keep up. The Fail Whale image, signifying a site crash, appeared too often in the early days. The company was also slow to formulate a plan for raising revenue.

SUCCESSES

Twitter has become a global information network, breaking major news stories around the world and allowing people to keep connected with one another. The company has attracted major celebrities and businesses as subscribers and raised more than a billion dollars in investments.

IMPACT ON SOCIETY

Twitter no longer is merely a mass of reports on what subscribers had for breakfast. Users are spreading vital news about world events as they happen, organizing protests, making professional connections, as well as keeping tabs on their favorite celebrities. Twitter users have become one big bustling interconnected community just as Jack Dorsey imagined.

QUOTE

"In short, the most fascinating thing about Twitter is not what it's doing to us. It's what we're doing to it."

—*Steve Johnson,* Time *magazine, June 5, 2009*

GLOSSARY

application

Computer software designed to help the user perform tasks.

dispatch

Sending an emergency vehicle, courier, or taxi to a specific location.

feed

An ongoing stream of Twitter messages.

follow

The means on Twitter by which a subscriber signs up to view other subscribers' updates.

handle

The username a Twitter user has selected and the accompanying URL, that is, http://twitter.com/username.

memory

Where data and program information is stored on a computer for later retrieval and use.

modem

An electronic device that transmits data from one computer to another via phone lines.

podcast
> A music or talk program available in a digital format that can be downloaded over the Internet.

Short Message Service (SMS)
> The technology behind text messaging on phones and other mobile communications systems.

smartphone
> A mobile phone with computerlike features including e-mail, Internet, and a personal organizer.

social media
> Web sites, applications, and content shared on social networks and other user-generated sites.

software
> The programs used to direct the operations of a computer.

ADDITIONAL RESOURCES

SELECTED BIBLIOGRAPHY

Carlson, Nicholas. "The Real History of Twitter." *Business Insider.* Business Insider, 13 Apr. 2011. Web. 15 Dec. 2011.

Kirkpatrick, David, "Twitter Was Act One: Jack Dorsey," *Vanity Fair*. Vanity Fair, Apr. 2011. Web. 15 Dec. 2011.

O'Reilly, Tim, and Sarah Milstein. *The Twitter Book*. Sebastopol, CA: O'Reilly Media, 2009. Print.

Safko, Lon. *The Social Media Bible: Tactics, Tools and Strategies for Business Success*. Hoboken, NJ: Wiley, 2010. Print.

Sagolla, Dom. *140 Characters: A Style Guide to the Short Form*. Hoboken, NJ: Wiley, 2009. Print.

FURTHER READINGS

Hamen, Susan E. *Google: The Company and Its Founders.* Minneapolis, MN: Abdo, 2011. Print.

Lusted, Marcia Amidon. *Mark Zuckerberg: Facebook Creator*. Minneapolis, MN: Abdo, 2011. Print.

Lusted, Marcia Amidon. *Social Networking: MySpace, Facebook, & Twitter*. Minneapolis, MN: Abdo, 2011. Print.

WEB LINKS

To learn more about Twitter, visit ABDO Publishing Company online at **www.abdopublishing.com.** Web sites about Twitter are featured on our Book Links page. These links are routinely monitored and updated to provide the most current information available.

PLACES TO VISIT

Computer History Museum
1401 North Shoreline Boulevard, Mountain View, CA 94043
650-810-1010
http://www.computerhistory.org
The Computer History Museum is the world's premier museum documenting and exploring the history of computing and its impact on society.

Twitter Headquarters
1355 Market Street, San Francisco, CA 94103
http://www.twitter.com
Twitter plans to move into its new headquarters in mid-2012.

SOURCE NOTES

CHAPTER 1. BREAKING NEWS
1. Claudine Beaumont. "New York Plane Crash: Twitter Breaks the News Again." *The Telegraph*. Telegraph Media Group, 16 Jan. 2009. Web. 15 Dec. 2011.

2. "Sullenberger Recalls Moment Engines Died." *60 Minutes*. CBS News, 10 March 2009. Web. 15 Dec. 2011.

3. Susan Young. "5 Lessons on Citizen Journalism." *Get in Front Communications*. Get in Front Communications, 29 Oct. 2010. Web. 15 Dec. 2011.

4. Ibid.

5. Claudine Beaumont. "New York Plane Crash: Twitter Breaks the News Again." *The Telegraph*. Telegraph Media Group, Jan. 16, 2009. Web. 15 Dec. 2011.

6. "Definition of 'Twitter.'" *Dictionary.com*. Dictionary.com. Web. 15 Dec. 2011.

7. Jack Dorsey (jack). "just setting up my twttr." 21 March 2006. Tweet. 15 Dec. 2011.

8. Biz Stone. "What's Happening?" *Twitter Blog*. Twitter, 19 Nov. 2009. Web. 15 Dec. 2011.

9. Susan Young. "5 Lessons on Citizen Journalism." *Get in Front Communications*. Get in Front Communications, 29 Oct. 2010. Web. 15 Dec. 2011.

CHAPTER 2. BEFORE TWITTER
None.

CHAPTER 3. FROM TAXICABS TO TWEETS
1. David Kirkpatrick. "Twitter Was Act One." *Vanity Fair*. Vanity Fair, Apr. 2011. Web. 15 Dec. 2011.

2. "Exclusive Twitter Interview! Jack Dorsey Founder of Twitter and Square - Foundation." *Foundation*. YouTube, 3 Jan. 2011. Web. 15 Dec. 2011.

3. David Kirkpatrick. "Twitter Was Act One." *Vanity Fair*. Vanity Fair, Apr. 2011. Web. 15 Dec. 2011.

4. "Exclusive Twitter Interview! Jack Dorsey Founder of Twitter and Square - Foundation." *Foundation*. YouTube, 3 Jan. 2011. Web. 15 Dec. 2011.

5. David Kirkpatrick. "Twitter Was Act One." *Vanity Fair*. Vanity Fair, April 2011. Web. 15 Dec. 2011.

6. Ibid.

CHAPTER 4. EVAN WILLIAMS AND BIZ STONE
1. Claire Cain Miller. "Why Twitter's C.E.O. Demoted Himself." *New York Times*. New York Times, 30 Oct. 2010. Web. 12 March 2012.

2. Evan Williams. "For Twitter C.E.O., Well-Orchestrated Accidents." *New York Times*. New York Times, 7 Mar. 2009. Web. 12 March 2012.

3. Ibid.

4. Ibid.

5. Claire Cain Miller. "Why Twitter's C.E.O. Demoted Himself." *New York Times*. New York Times, 30 Oct. 2010. Web. 12 Mar. 2012.

6. Carolyne Zinko. "What Is Biz Stone Doing?" *San Francisco Chronicle*. Hearst Communications, 5 April 2009. Web. 12 Mar. 2012.

7. Ibid.

8. Ibid.

9. Michael S. Malone. "The Twitter Revolution." *Wall Street Journal*. Wall Street Journal, 18 April 2009. Web. 12 Mar. 2012.

10. Biz Stone. *Who Let the Blogs Out?: A Hyperconnected Peek at the World of Weblogs*. New York: Macmillan, 2004. Print. Introduction.

11. Mimi Towle. "Biz Stone." *Marin Magazine*. Open Sky Media, Aug. 2010. Web. 12 Mar. 2012.

12. Courtney Hoffman. "It's Not Easy Being Biz." *Reuters*. Thomson Reuters, 18 May 2009. Web. 12 Mar. 2012.

13. Mimi Towle. "Biz Stone." *Marin Magazine*. Open Sky Media, Aug. 2010. Web. 12 Mar. 2012.

14. "Exclusive Twitter Interview! Jack Dorsey Founder of Twitter and Square - Foundation." *Foundation*. YouTube, 3 Jan. 2011. Web. 15 Dec. 2011.

CHAPTER 5. FOLLOW THE LEADER

1. Nicholas Carlson. "The Real History of Twitter." *Business Insider*. Business Insider, 13 Apr. 2011. Web. 15 Dec. 2011.

2. Ibid.

3. Ibid.

4. Michael Arrington. "Odeo Releases Twttr." *TechCrunch*. AOL Tech, 15 July 2006. Web. 15 Dec. 2011.

5. Ibid.

6. Nicholas Carlson. "The Real History of Twitter." *Business Insider*. Business Insider, 13 Apr. 2011. Web. 15 Dec. 2011.

7. Ibid.

8. Om Malik. "RIP Odeo, Hello Obvious Corp." *Gigaom Blog*. GigaOM, 25 Oct. 2006. Web. 15 Dec. 2011.

9. Evan Williams. "The Birth of Obvious Corp." *evhead Blog*. Evan Williams, 25 Oct. 2006. Web. 15 Dec. 2011.

10. Maureen Dowd. "To Tweet or Not to Tweet." *New York Times*. New York Times, 22 Apr. 2009. Web. 15 Dec. 2011.

11. Nicholas Carlson. "The Real History of Twitter." *Business Insider*. Business Insider, 13 Apr. 2011. Web. 15 Dec. 2011.

12. Steve Johnson. "How Twitter Will Change the Way We Live." *Time*. Time, 5 June 2009. Web. 15 Dec. 2011.

13. Ibid.

SOURCE NOTES CONTINUED

CHAPTER 6. ENCOURAGING SIGNS AND GROWING PAINS

1. Taylor Barnes. "Haiti Earthquake: Twitter Offers Glimpse of the Scene, Lifeline of Hope." *Christian Science Monitor*. Christian Science Monitor, 13 Jan. 2010. Web. 15 Dec. 2011.

2. Nicholas Carlson. "Twitter's Road to $1 Billion." *Business Insider*. Business Insider, 30 Sept. 2009. Web. 15 Dec. 2011.

3. Heather Green. "Twitter: All Trivia, All The Time." *BusinessWeek*. Bloomberg, 2 Apr. 2007. Web. 15 Dec. 2011.

4. Ibid.

5. David Kirkpatrick. "Twitter Was Act One." *Vanity Fair*. Vanity Fair, Apr. 2011. Web. 15 Dec. 2011.

6. Tim O'Reilly and Sarah Milstein. *The Twitter Book*. Sebastopol, CA: O'Reilly Media, Inc., 2009. Print. 53.

7. David Kirkpatrick. "Twitter Was Act One." *Vanity Fair*. Vanity Fair, April 2011. Web. 15 Dec. 2011.

8. Matt Forsythe. "Interview with 'Fail Whale' Artist, Yiying Lu." *Drawn*. Drawn, 21 July 2008. Web. 15 Dec. 2011.

9. David Kirkpatrick. "Twitter Was Act One." *Vanity Fair*. Vanity Fair, Apr. 2011. Web. 15 Dec. 2011.

10. Nicholas Carlson. "Twitter's Road to $1 Billion." *Business Insider*. Business Insider, 30 Sept. 2009. Web. 15 Dec. 2011.

11. Claire Cain Miller. "Why Twitter's C.E.O. Demoted Himself." *New York Times*. New York Times, 30 Oct. 2010. Web. 12 March 2012.

12. Nicholas Carlson. "Twitter's Road to $1 Billion." *Business Insider*. Business Insider, 30 Sept. 2009. Web. 15 Dec. 2011.

CHAPTER 7. TWEET, TWEET LITTLE STAR

1. Dan Frommer. "Celebrities Take Over Twitter, Kick Geeks Aside." *Business Insider*. Business Insider, 17 April 2009. Web. 15 Dec. 2011.

2. Ashton Kutcher. "The Twitter Guys." *Time*. Time, 30 April 2009. Web. 15 Dec. 2011.

3. Tim O'Reilly and Sarah Milstein. *The Twitter Book*. Sebastopol, CA: O'Reilly Media, Inc., 2009. Print. 17.

4. Lauren Dugan. "Is Twitter Dumbing Down English, Like Ralph Fiennes Thinks?" *All Twitter at Media Bistro*. WebMediaBrands, 28 Oct. 2011. Web. 15 Dec. 2011.

5. Lauren Dugan. "Literary Legend Margaret Atwood Thinks Twitter Boosts Literacy." *All Twitter at Media Bistro*. WebMediaBrands, 6 Dec. 2011. Web. 15 Dec. 2011.

6. Ibid.

7. Vanessa Grigoriadis. "America's Tweethearts." *Vanity Fair*. Vanity Fair, Feb. 2010. Web. 15 Dec. 2011.

8. Alexis Madrigal. "Revealing the Man Behind @MayorEmanuel." *The Atlantic*. Atlantic Monthly, 28 Feb. 2011. Web. 15 Dec. 2011.

CHAPTER 8. LIVE-TWEETING HISTORY

1. Jolie O'Dell. "One Twitter User Reports Live From Osama Bin Laden Raid." *Mashable*. Mashable, 2 May 2011. Web. 15 Dec. 2011.

2. Ibid.

3. Ibid.

4. Ibid.

5. Anna Applebaum. "Egypt's Uprising Should Be Encouraged." *Washington Post*. Washington Post, 31 Jan. 2011. Web. 15 Dec. 2011.

6. Jared Keller. "Evaluating Iran's Twitter Revolution." *The Atlantic*. Atlantic Monthly, 18 June 2010. Web. 15 Dec. 2011.

7. Bill Wasik. "#Riot: Self-Organized, Hyper-Networked Revolts—Coming to a City Near You." *Wired*. Condé Nast, 16 Dec. 2011. Web. 1 May 2012.

8. Ibid.

9. Ibid.

CHAPTER 9. THE FUTURE OF TWITTER

1. Lauren Dugan. "Twitter Sees 4 Billion SMS Per Month, Expects Much More Growth." *All Twitter at Media Bistro*. WebMediaBrands, 28 Sept. 2011. Web. 15 Dec. 2011.

2. Evan Williams. "An Obvious Next Step." *evhead Blog*. Evan Williams, 29 Mar. 2011. Web. 15 Dec. 2011.

3. Ibid.

4. Biz Stone. "It's So Obvious." *Biz Stone's Blog*. Biz Stone, 28 June 2011. Web. 15 Dec. 2011.

5. Ibid.

6. Jessica Guynn. "Twitter CEO Dick Costolo Is Determined to Get the Last Laugh." *Chicago Tribune*. Chicago Tribue, 6 Feb. 2011. Web. 15 Dec. 2011.

7. Evan Williams. "An Obvious Next Step," *evhead Blog*. Evan Williams, 29 Mar. 2011. Web. 15 Dec. 2011.

8. "200 Million Tweets Per Day." *Twitter Blog*. Twitter, 30 June 2011. Web. 15 Dec. 2011.

9. Biz Stone. "It's So Obvious." *Biz Stone's Blog*. Biz Stone, 28 June 2011. Web. 15 Dec. 2011.

10. Liz Gannes. "Twitter Redesigns to be Simpler and Faster." *All Things D*. All Things D, 8 Dec. 2011. Web. 15 Dec. 2011.

11. "Yours to Discover: A Faster, Simpler Way to Stay Close to Everything You Care About." *Twitter*. Twitter, 2011. Web. 15 Dec. 2011.

12. Liz Gannes. "Twitter Redesigns to be Simpler and Faster." *All Things D*. All Things D, 8 Dec. 2011. Web. 15 Dec. 2011.

INDEX

ABOUT THE AUTHOR

Christine Heppermann is a columnist and reviewer for the *Horn Book Magazine*. She has contributed chapters to *A Family of Readers: The Book Lover's Guide to Children's and Young Adult Literature* and *Children's Books and Their Creators*. She has also written a nonfiction picture book and has published poetry in literary journals for adults. Heppermann has an MA in children's literature from Simmons College and an MFA in writing for children and young adults from Hamline University.

PHOTO CREDITS

Gabriela Hasbun/Aurora Photos/Alamy, cover; Janis Krums, 6; Kajdi Szabolcs/iStockphoto, 9; Jeff Chiu/AP Images, 13; Mark Lennihan/AP Images, 15; AP Images, 16; Matt Sayles/AP Images, 18; Günay Mutlu/iStockphoto, 23; meshaphoto/iStockphoto, 24; SSPL/Getty Images, 26; Jeff Chiu/AP Images, 31; Charles Sykes/AP Images, 99 (bottom); Paul Sakuma/AP Images, 34; Jen Grantham/iStockphoto, 38, 97 (top); Kimberly White/Reuters, 40; Eric Risberg/AP Images, 45, 96; Wayne Howes/Shutterstock Images, 46, 97 (bottom); Matt Sayles/AP Images, 49; Elena Elisseeva/Shutterstock Images, 57; Tomasz Pietryszek/iStockphoto, 58; David Robertson/Alamy, 62; Charles Dharapak/AP Images, 67; Jemal Countess/WireImage/Getty Images, 68; Helga Esteb/Shutterstock Images, 71; Alexander Zemlianichenko/AP Images, 73, 99 (top); Charles Rex Arbogast/AP Images, 77; David Loh/Reuters, 78; MOHPhoto/Shutterstock, 82; Maya Alleruzzo/AP Images, 85; Michael Loccisano/Getty Images for Time Warner/Getty Images, 86; Bloomberg/Getty Images, 91; Jeff Chiu/AP Images, 92; Manu Fernandez/AP Images, 95, 98